PEACE TALKS

Peace Talks

ANDR

FABER & FABER

First published in 2015
by Faber & Faber Ltd
Bloomsbury House
74–77 Great Russell Street
London WC1B 3DA
This paperback edition first published in 2016

Typeset by Hamish Ironside
Printed in England by Martins the Printers, Berwick-upon-Tweed

A CIP record for this book
is available from the British Library

ISBN 978–0–571–32548–1

MIX
Paper from
responsible sources
FSC® C013254
www.fsc.org

10 9 8 7 6 5 4 3 2 1

for Kyeong-Soo

Contents

Affectus, qui passio est, desinit esse passio simulatque eius claram et distinctam formamus ideam.
SPINOZA, *Ethics*

I MY OWN BLUE EYE

The Discoveries of Geography

If only the stories were not so tempting –
but from day one I started to embroider,
and in no time was suggesting a country
far to the north
where fish are as large as dragons,
and even minor administrators
eat off gold plates,
and sleep on gold beds.

This is why I have packed in my birch canoe
a robe
made of the feathers
of more than a hundred different species of bird.

So that when I have finally crossed the ocean
I will have a ceremonial costume
rich enough
to impress in my encounter with the Great Khan.

*

We have an excellent long boat with outriggers
and therefore travel dozens of miles in a day.

Furthermore, and speaking as a navigator,
I can predict every fickleness of weather
and also the change in direction of currents,
sometimes dipping my elbow into the water
and sometimes my scrotum
to feel the slightest change in temperature.

These are the reasons
I shall be considered a saviour by my people
and die in peace.

In my own mind I am a simple man
who threw his spear at the stars
and landed there himself.

*

I now have in my possession
a map:
two handfuls of mud
scraped from the bank of our sacred river,
flattened into a tablet,
baked,
then pierced with the blunt point of my compass
while I spun the other sharper leg
to produce the edge of the world as I knew it,

and beyond
the salt sea on which I am now perfectly at home.

In this way I look down at myself.

I think: I am here.

*

Astonishing, how many horizons are open to me:

at one time mountainous heaps of smashed slate,

at others a vast delta of green and crimson light.

And every day a different shoreline ripples past
bearing its cargo of white sand and dark palms.

Very beguiling they appear, but all encumbered.
All spoiled by the tantrums of their local gods.

Out here there are storms too,
but in the religion I have now devised for myself,
I am convinced
the shaping hands have pulled away from us at last,
so the Earth hangs with no support at the centre of –
what?
That is the question I have in mind to answer.

*

You might suppose better charts would help me,
but despite their much greater accuracy

in terms of coastlines and interiors,

and the intricate detail
guaranteed by developments in printing,

not to mention the understanding of perspective,

empires still lie about their extent and stability.

These are the simple deceptions.

More difficult,
as I continue north to my final encounter,
and wave-crests flicking my face grow colder
and daylight a more persistently dull dove-grey,
is how to manage my desire to live in the present
for all eternity,
as though I had never left my home.

*

It transpires the last part of my journey
requires me to abandon everything I once knew,
even the gorgeous costume
made of the feathers of more than a hundred different
    species of bird.

No matter, though.
It is delicious among the constellations,
as the planets begin to display their gas-clouds
and the beautiful nebulae their first attempts at stars,

When I look over my shoulder
to see my own blue eye staring back at me,
I realise before I disappear
I still accept what it means to be lost.

The Conclusion of Joseph Turrill

Garsington, Oxfordshire, 1867

I suppose I was cut out for a quiet life;
whether I have managed any such thing
is another matter,
what with larks to shoot,
and harvesting, gooseberries, and whatnot.

Then there was all that with Netty:
would she or wouldn't she;
did I or didn't I?
It is my belief
I spent more hours kicking my heels at her gate
than happy the other side.

Be that as it may.
Anno Domini drives out stern matters of fact,
and faults that appear to us
when we compare the lives we have
with those we imagine . . .
There's nothing a gentle stroll
in the woods by moonlight can't put right.

I tried that just now.
I saw swallows on the branches like clothes pegs,
which put me in such good humour
I brought home one of their nests and also four chicks.

An Echidna for Chris Wallace-Crabbe

Whatever kind of determination a creature needs
to enjoy one state of existence before confronting the next,
the echidna has a-plenty.

Look how the legs which once upon a time were fins,

then paddles,

and now are covered with spines as delicate as fur,

shunt this specimen up the barren mound
that forms the one significant feature of his pen,
still hampered by the excessive weight of his body
but clearly not enough
to feel distracted from his main ambition.

Which is to reach this particular point
by the concrete wall that marks the limit of his freedom,
where he shovels the earth aside with his rubber snout
before giving up when roughly half submerged.

He has no idea
anyone is waiting for him at the end of history.

But he obviously understands
that to start again at the beginning
and change faster
would only mean taking the straight road to extinction.

A Meeting of Minds with Henry David Thoreau

1 Into the Wood

When I arrived in that new country for the first time
    I came by boat
by canoe in fact
        and completely alone
so the pines and conifers
    stepping down to the river
        some with their roots
            as pink as pigs' tails
in the dark current swirling around them
    were my only company.

It was for this reason I found myself
        striking my double-ended paddle
hard against the side of my canoe
    to frighten them away
if such a thing were possible.

To start echoes
    and have those echoes
        multiply
and fill the woods
        with circles of dilating sound
awakening the trees.

    Stirring up I call it
as might be done
        to animals and people.

To make all melodies a replica
    of the things they give a voice
        and the places where I find them.

2 *Finds*

Their spears are very serviceable
    the pointed part a hemlock knot
        and the side-spring
            pieces of hickory
    for use on salmon
        pickerel
        trout
        chub
        etc.
unless
    by the light of birch-fires after sunset
        it is converted into a pole or club.

These were my first discoveries.

After that
a sled   or *jebongon*
    carved from thin wood
turned up at the front
        and drawn by a strong bark rope.

A cradle.

    A canoe
        much more convenient than my own.

A vessel for water
        or for boiling meat with hot stones.

And arrow-heads
    that lie through the woods like expectation
        over the whole face of America.

Stone fruit I thought
  but soon afterwards
frost flowers
    that still appear to my eye
      and are cold to my touch
when the frost itself wears off
  and the ground is bare.

3 *Travellers*

I planted out the first potatoes today
    when I was not reading
        F. A. Michaux
        the younger Michaux that is
describing himself on the shore of the Monongahela

    as five or six bateaux filled with horses
    cattle
    pigs
    poultry
    dismounted carts
    ploughs
    harnesses and beds
presented in turn their ends
        their sides
            their burrowing prows
to the current that swept them on
                towards their destination.

To think of so many arriving
    put me in mind of a friend
who recently broke into the grasslands
    and was impeded for a day
by a herd of bison
    fifty miles long
        and three miles wide.

When he followed them to a ford
    the gravel underfoot
            was covered with moulted hair
            to a depth of
                    six inches.

4 *The Axe*

I threw my axe behind me
    towards the lake
and being filled with the involuntary life of things
    it skimmed some twenty yards across the ice
        and then dropped in
through a hole I had recently made there myself.

I crawled back out
    and saw it twenty-five feet down
        the handle upright
        swaying in the bright clear water
        as if the water or the axe itself
had discovered a pulse.

Which decided me.

I made a device of birch and rope
    hooked the axe after several attempts
        raised it
        seized it
and brought it home.

In my absence
I had missed two visitors
    or so their footprints told me.

One left me nothing I could know them by.

The other
    might have been a woman
        judging by the gift

of wood-shavings and pale grasses
    picked before the snow
        and twisted now
in a bouquet that lingered on my table.

5 *Cobwebs*

Because I had already chosen

    the hawk who would not leave her nest

    and the snapping turtle whose head is big as a child
but terrible as a crocodile

    and the owl who turned to stone
when I paddled under the hemlock bank

    and the baskets of wild cranberry and huckleberry

I crept out this morning to see the gossamer webs
    extending from my clear ground
        towards a stand of black willows
            they had completely covered up
with lines in parallel

    not taut
        but curving downwards in the middle
            like the rigging of tall ships
that swoops from mast to mast

    as if a thousand nations had collected
        but were going nowhere
            and content with that.

6 *The River*

Although I have heard

    or could not help myself imagining
        in quieter times

the railway with its clink and flutter
    not to mention the lanes and highways

I always planned to leave these woods
    by following the river as I came.

    Today
the geese that rise to see me off
    will also take its course
        but only roughly
            cutting short the twists and turns.

I confine myself

    and choose the slow meander of the current

    the long reflections of the trees

    the trees themselves
        beech and pine and conifer

    the echoes which
as they die out behind me
        sound like water running
            backwards to its source
to start again.

The Death of George Mallory and Sandy Irvine

When the time came to see them off
I dressed laboriously in a wool vest and long drawers,

a shirt and two sweaters,

comfortable knickerbockers made of windproof gabardine,

a pair of soft elastic Kashmir putties,

ankle-boots soled with English leather
and nailed with Alpine nails,

a fur-lined cycling helmet, goggles,

and a leather mask covering every part of my face
not protected by my beard.

A thick grey hand-knitted muffler completed the costume.

*

After we had shaken hands
I can only imagine the two of them left at their usual quick
     pace
and soon vanished among the monstrous snow-humps
and ice-crevasses that led towards the peak.

I do not remember seeing this.

I can say, however,
that when I abandoned the Northeast Shoulder
and drifted over the North Face,

where I noticed a variety of highly altered limestones
and also the igneous intrusions of lighter granitic rocks,

I found a crag standing one hundred feet tall
and decided to test my condition by climbing to the top.

As I reached my goal the sky lifted,
the mist blew away,
and I glimpsed the Northeast Ridge and the Summit itself.

My eyes became fixed on a minute black speck
silhouetted against a smooth snow-crest
beneath a rock-step on the ridge.

Then this vision disappeared from view
in typically heavy white clouds.

*

Shortly afterwards the weather closed in,
a pressure-drop so severe
it squeezed the breath from my body.

It was late afternoon,
and I knew that even if they managed
to conquer the six hundred and fifty feet they needed
to reach the Summit,
returning would be another matter.

I therefore decided to help them
when they began their descent,
climbing until I encountered their camp
as visibility shrank to zero.

Their tent was empty.

After searching it for proof
of what they had meant to do,
I stepped back into the gale
and continued my search

for another three or four hours,
repeatedly shouting their names
as loudly as possible across the wilderness.

Eventually I went back to the tent again
and dragged outside their sleeping bags
to make an X in the snow.

*

After two more days
and no further evidence
I began my own descent,

clambering through treacherous iceberg scenery at first,
then discovering a good moraine track
that led me down into valleys filled with flowers
and so to our Base Camp.

In my final estimation
the mountain looked very beautiful,
and I decided my friends
must have been enchanted in the same way.

It was the beginning of their mystery
and no mystery at all.

I can think of no better way to explain
why they chose to stay.

The Concern: Samuel Taylor Coleridge and William Wordsworth

One has tramped forty miles, but at the sight
below him vaults the gate into standing wheat
and, with the hard heads rasping against him,
bounds forward taking for once a straight line
rather than musing roundabout, while the other
stops digging the vegetable rows in his garden
to watch this face which will persist in vanishing
then rising in the sea of green becoming gold.

*

This face is the face of an angel already falling,
the mouth open, voluptuous, gross, eloquent;
the chin good-humoured and round; the nose,
the rudder, small, feeble, nothing. But dramatic.
The other is gaunt, internal, plain, solemn, lyrical,
not yet stony from effort of suffering, although
thrust beyond the pale of love already, his likings
running along new channels, the old ones dry.

*

Old things have passed away, and new violence –
the rage and dog-day heat – that has died out too.
One says at the fireside: I am no longer for public life;
I have snapped my squeaking baby-trumpet of sedition.
Meanwhile the other, woken by this strange tenderness,
breaks the silence in himself. He thinks it is possible
now to describe the attraction of a country in romance,
and reasonable to live like a green leaf on the blessed tree.

*

Briefly to all intents and purposes they are one man
joined to the other – they have become one another –
Mr Colesworth or Wordridge, the Concern, settling
here at the hard roadside in the guise of a vagrant,
or there unfolding into an albatross and skimming
over the shining masts and slavers of Bristol docks
as if they were both one sailor who fell overboard;
a lost soul labouring north towards the ice and sun.

*

Then they find and make their chosen resort a fold
where a stream falls down a sloping wall of rock
to form a waterfall considerable for this country,
and across the pool: an ash tree, with its branches
spindling up in search of light. For want of that
the shaking leaves have faded almost lily-white,
while downwards from the trunk hang ivy-trails
a-sway to prove the breathing of the waterfall.

*

This is a fine place to talk treason, if not a place
to forget there is any need for treason. And yet,
sequestered as it might be in wild Poesy, the mind
still becomes illegible to itself for no good reason.
And yet, external things will lose the sense of having
their external life, and men that cannot fly will grow
and stretch their wings in the abyss of their ideals,
and grieve that all they have is just the feel of flight.

*

One says nothing. The other says: two giants leagued
together, their names are called BREAD & CHEESE.
The other says nothing. One says: my past life seems
to me like a dream, a feverish dream! all one gloomy
huddle of strange actions and dim-coloured motives!
The other says nothing. One says: it is a painful idea
that our existence is of very little use; I have left
my friends, I have left plenty. The other says nothing.

Before the Court

at the Foundling Hospital

We fall
      and everyone
we fall

      what makes you
with your flowing plaster   and
      your swag   your little
eyelet pictures   and

the boys here in the hospital
      the marbles   and
forbid them not

we fall   we fall   and look

green rushes O   green rushes
      where the current brought him
where
      no matter   I

I am a woman of good character.

Two Late Portraits

1 Audrey Wills

I was a Brixham girl
and Dad's boat was
    the pride of the fleet

every day
    when they came ashore
        I had my pick of the mackerel
        beautiful
            shiny blue suits

then again
    I was stationed on the flying boats
that was a lovely time
they came in   very low over the water
    or seemed to

ask yourself
    what will you remember

in Llandudno   on honeymoon
singing at night   can you hear me
singing   and
I painted my toenails red
    I still do this
        by myself
that's me there
dancing round and round the house
without a single brown penny in my purse

you see what I am saying
    I am living
every colour except grey

    and   you would not believe
        I have
looked after everyone   O
but I have
    when I go to the doctor now
        I find the door   closed
            do I knock   what
do I do

I sing

come in   I am Richard   I landed
on Gold Beach   I am Peter
        I was married to Steve for fifty-seven years
            I am Helen aged seventy-two
                and I do tatting
        I am Ali a widow   I am Ron
and I enjoy boiled potatoes
    and a drop of broth
        I am not a lover of sweet things

as for me   I am Audrey   Audrey   open
    the window
        and let me hear the seagulls
            let me hear the seagulls flying across

as for me   I love God and   I want to die
    what better thing is there   to live for

2 *Sheila Smith*

Is there anybody there   O
     Nobby   our Suffolk   what
Suffolk Punch   poor Nobby   he
trod on a wasps' nest
but it's bone   it's only bone

     we led him
to and fro in the harvest time
     Michael and me
         first field then barn
in harvest time   my brother and me

and next   what's red   bright red
     the tractor   yes   poor Nobby
           well

I saw Aunt Mary cut him up
     she cut him up
she sliced him in her kitchen with the flags
     and blood
blood ran over her elbows
     all in the High Street   Number 11

here it is now   see   Nobby
his painless foot   my horse
     champed in the silence   champed
         the forest's ferny floor

no it's my father   O
   here's my father walking down the stairs
      don't fall
         don't miss your step you

don't forget
      the silence surging softly
Michael in his arms   but limp
   then out

and so
   I step aside   aged twelve   I do
I stand aside and let them pass

I watch my brother carried to the car
I do
     is anyone   is anyone   is there
the Traveller said

The Realms of Gold

In a quiet part of Leamington Spa
in the same flat
where he has lived all his life,
sixty-two-year-old Michael Standage
is close to completing his biography
of the poet D. J. Enright.

Nobody reads Enright now
apart from a few surviving friends
and a handful of fans
who insist he is under-rated.

Standage does not speak to them.

He is nervous of an interpretation
that differs from his own,
and they are jealous of him;
it's not as though his book
is authorised or anything;
he just got there first
and found that archive in Japan.

All the same Standage
is confident of a clear run home.
He works late each night
and only pauses
to watch a black wind
stirring the trees that line his side street
but stop
where it meets the main road.

*

Meanwhile the poems of D. J. Enright
gather dust in second-hand bookshops
or fly into a skip
along with other unwanted things
that go when a life ends.

A long history of adventure and homecoming.

A fastidious editor yet free
to travel in the realms of gold.

A highly original mind
with Proust among others
virtually off by heart.

And speaking of the heart . . .

But to date only Standage can do that
with any confidence.

The rest of us, the few
of us,
open the dark green *Collected* and think:
this was a life as good as any;
who am I to let it vanish completely
without returning an echo.

When I read him and I listen
to the silence following,
I know
exactly what he means.

*

Standage makes an exception to his rule
and accepts my invitation to meet.

We decide on Brighton,
which is neutral ground,
and walk for an hour on the shingle.

Following publication
can we look forward
to a revival of Enright's fortunes?

We both sincerely hope so
and, while the dry grey stones
grind under our shoes,
extol the virtues for which we feel
a common admiration,
especially as they appear
in *Paradise Illustrated*
and *The Terrible Shears*.

Once we have reached our climax
we stand still
and stare out to sea.

Small waves beat towards us,
fold over neatly, and turn into foam.

Very soon more follow and
the same thing happens.

Three Witnesses

1 *The Wilderness*

What does a man see
    in the wilderness
        if not a reed
shaken by the wind.

Since I arrived here
I have admired thousands
    for the music they produce

astringent in summer
    in winter fuller
        and more nearly sweet
thanks to the green moisture in the leaf.

As for human visitors
    there has only been
        this stranger
who
    if he spoke at all
argued with his shadow.

So far as I can tell
    nothing changed when he went.

I still bathe in the streams
poured out by the desert lark.

I still read the news I need
    in the footprints of lizards
    and the looping hieroglyphics
snakes leave with their skin.

2 *Lazarus*

I slipped over the border.

I fell down
    in the pure dark
        with no dreaming.

Then I came home again.

Wherever I go now
    to market in the village
        or working the fields at harvest
I prefer to imagine
    I leave footprints of swirling light.

In truth
    there is nothing so obvious
to show I am unlike
    the man I was before.

And yet
    to speak in confidence
I am almost worn through
        by the terms of my existence.

They require me
    to raise my voice
        every   single   day

and declare that I am happy.

3 *The Upper Room*

My task is to clear the room
when the guests go home at night.

To straighten the benches

to sweep up the breadcrumbs
        fish skeletons
                and pepper stalks

to separate the olives from the olive stones

and
        to wipe away the stain
                if any wine has spilt
between the pitcher
                and the cups.

A Fight in Poland

Beyond the outskirts of Gdańsk
where the docklands and factories expire
in a shimmering wasteland
of foul-smelling marshes and black creeks,
and the Baltic Sea chews over its sorrows
never attempting to resolve them,
I came to a hotel as big as a palace.

The lobby

was like the interior of a gun-case,
darkened with red velvet that a clever workman
had pressed over mouldings and cornices;

my room

when I reached it along freezing corridors
where the timber groaned beneath me,
was simple as a hermit's cell,
with a view across sand dunes
to the dark brown Baltic shoreline.

I was saturated.

I had no change of clothes.

But the shower worked after a fashion,
and an hour later I presented myself in the restaurant
where waiters slid very smoothly between the empty tables,
but still managed to rattle the cutlery,
and shake a faint musical accompaniment
from the throats of wine glasses.

I had eel.

Six inches of shining green eel
and a bottle of white rioja.

Enough to send me upstairs in due course
thinking I had drunk the electric Baltic,
which I saw from the window on the stairway
was still fizzing under a fierce barrage of rain.

After an hour's sleep or strong hallucination
I was woken by the sound of two men
fighting in the adjacent room.
Heavy, muscular men
pounding each other with their fists,
and afterwards heaving together on a bed
before finishing with that
and throwing down on the bare floor
a wardrobe,
a mirror,
several books,
then one glass followed by another glass.

I grew used to the disturbance.

So completely used to it, in fact,
I did not even turn a hair
when the door from their room into mine
bulged on its golden hinges,
and debated whether to break open.

For this reason I said nothing next morning
as I took my place in the dining room
now flooded with cold white light
streaming in off the Baltic.

And nothing again
as the waiter poured out my coffee
and the hotel slipped her moorings.

We set forth over waves
heading due North,
and I still remained seated at my table;
I expected my neighbours from the night before
would appear at any minute
and introduce themselves.

But they must have disembarked already,
and I soon forgot them.

I was concentrating now on the icebergs
as they sailed past my window.

The icebergs, and the whales
that always let fly with a water-spout
before they bent below the surface.

The Fish in Australia

Where the mountains crumbled
and yellow desert began,
when the sun began to smoulder
in a vault of indigo,
I left the metalled road
and found a perfect circle
of still and silent water
fifty yards across,
with hard treeless banks
unmarked by any prints.

Call it a pool of tears
wept by dogs and kangaroos,
or dead transported men.
I considered it a dew pond
but no dew anywhere
ever fell that swarthy colour,
or seemed so like the lid
of a tunnel piercing through
the planet's fiery heart
to the other side and England.

Providence anyhow
had made me think ahead
and without a moment's pause
I was parked up on the bank,
had my rod and spinner ready,
and was flicking out a cast
to find what rose to me.

Nothing rose of course.
A kookaburra guffawed
a mile off in the bush
and a million years ago;
a snack of tiny flies
sizzled round my lips;
and as the dying sun
sank deeper in its vault
a gang of eucalypts
in tattered party dresses
seemed to shuffle closer
and show their interest

in hearing how my line
whispered on the water
(now uniformly solid
ancient beaten bronze)
how the reel's neat click
made the spinner plonk down,
how the ratchet whirred
as I reeled in slow enough
to conjure up the monster
that surely slept below.

As I reeled in slow enough
then suddenly too slow
and the whirling hooks caught hold
of something obstinate.
Not flesh or fish-mouth though.
Too much dead weight for that.
A stone-age log perhaps.
A mass at any rate

that would not change its mind
and snapped the flimsy line
which blew back in my face
as light as human hair.

If not myself at least
the pond lay peaceful then,
with sun now turned to dust
and a moon-ghost in its place
as much like company
as anything complete.

Why not, I thought,
why not
despite the loss to me
continue standing here
and still cast out my line,
my frail and useless lash,
with no better reason now
than to watch the thing lie down
then lift and lie again,
until such time arrives
as the dark that swallowed up
the sky has swallowed me.

Swim

We quarrelled over something
    I don't remember
and   while you slept
I tried to make good
    by mending a broken pipe
    under the bathroom sink.

When I hit my head on the rim
I decided   to hell with it
    I'll spend the afternoon
taking a swim
        instead.

And why not
    prove myself
        capable after all
by ploughing across the harbour
    and back?

Given that meant   a mile
and all manner of shipping
    including a liner
    recently in from Barcelona
I had to strip off   and go
before I finished the question.

Breast-stroke
    crawl
        breast-stroke
    then for a while
floating
    getting my breath back

until the liner
        set sail for Barcelona again
which kept me treading water
    as long as the beast
        swung from the dockside
            out
    surprisingly quick   and yet
slow
    sloshing an oily ripple
        over my head as a joke
before
    looming above me
        capped with faces shouting
Look out!
    or
        Look!

I was still treading water
    treading
        water   but thinking
it will be time   soon
        to kick myself forward again
what with the liner
    sliding away from me now
    juggling the world in its wake
this way and that   then
    shouldering off
        through the harbour mouth.

        Achille Lauro
that was the name I saw.
        Achille Lauro.
            Wasn't it
captured by hijackers once

            didn't they
shoot   what was his name
            Klinghoffer
then tip him overboard
            out of his wheelchair?

I could return to that   I would
        later return to that   but now
I was halfway across   only
halfway across the harbour
        legs suddenly stringy
breath
            short
        and still   still a good way
        from starting the journey back.

What had I   ever   been thinking?
        What had I
            not been thinking?

You   I thought
            you will never need know
not if you
        never wake up.

It could be still
        an afternoon like the others
the lazy others we spend
        here on the island
in Caprichosa   in Cala Rata.

I might   really
        I might not remember
            how the enormous water
    opened beneath me

how
      a liner
    had easily slipped straight over
and through

how I swam onwards   a little
    rested
then swam onwards again
    until it was all
behind me
    all the silvery harbour
catching the light of late afternoon
    and I was back here in our bedroom again
      still lying beside you.

The Burning Car

Back from our swim in Es Grau
where nightingales
    sang from the pines
and a heron
         ignored us   priest
at his priestlike task
    in the freshwater pool
in Es Grau as I say
        the car caught fire.

A jalopy
but still   on fire
    a smudge
escaping the bonnet
        then feathers
the instrument panel
         then flame
the air-vents
the radio   glovebox
    the key in its slot
and out
    we jumped out
        in the sun
mesmerised though
      you could say mesmerised
       yes
         or baffled.

What did the universe need
            to explain?
Did it think
                we were stupid?

Well
we might have been stupid
                or worse
                        but at least
we were taking no chances
            keeping our distance
watching the tyres
        take hold
the windscreen
                        explode
then fire in a hurry
            guzzling
our damp front seats   the basket
            my towel
your red one   headrests
                        umbrella
our map of the island   sea holly
sweet wrappers
            lolly sticks   sand grains
                dust   dust
and your favourite hat
darling that too
            amazing how fast
                        how soon
in something we thought
                could never be burned
a car
            but was.

The Notary

For some reason
    were you
        selling your apartment
for some reason
    we needed a notary
so we uncoupled
    our holiday
and set about finding one.

The first step
    brought us down to the coast
as morning broke over Ravello
    through a comedy of hairpins
with our windows one minute
    scratched by savage brambles
        the next lit
    with a flash of the sea.

But the notaries of Amalfi
    were closed
        or spoke no English
    so on a second bus
we followed the coast road to Salerno
still with a good idea
    we might find what we wanted.

But the whole morning was now
    beauty thinning away
vine terraces and marble stairs
    veering
        among lavender rocks

and the other tourists
    disappearing as well
dropping off
    at the good bathing spots
or the last restaurant
    anyone had heard of
until it was just us
    and the other silent ones
who needed Salerno
    for their own business.

No one acknowledged us
    and
        everyone followed the view
religiously

the mountains to our left
    with profiles of old warriors
        and patchworks of myrtle
        gradually shrinking
as the pulses of lava that made them
    lost their vitality

the sea to our right
    sprinkled with white fishing boats
        furrowed by one blue ferry
    and whipped briefly by a helicopter
    that buzzed alongside us for half a mile
as if we were under surveillance
    or heading for danger.

Then the sky was empty again
    the road ahead straight and flat
and the music of our tyres
    playing over soft tarmac

the sunlight zithering through the blinds
     the heat scented with petrol fumes
          that swept in
               through open windows
were all peaceful enough
               all sleepy-making enough . . .

One minute there was no Salerno
     the next there were dockyards
     a port   suburbs   a ring-road
     a hideous ramshackle overpass
     marina   bridge   dual carriageway
     the Centro with its wide avenue of pines
and everything soaked through
     with a faint sour yellow
          version of
               colour-blindness.

We stepped down
     at the last stop before the depot
          and silence swallowed us like a marsh.
As it had swallowed already
     the first notary we tried
          and the next
               and the next
all
     at a tiresome distance
          from one another
          on long streets flanked
          with glaring concrete
where apart from a vagrant
     asleep on the veiny steps of a bank
          and a three-legged dog
          that made a point

             of hopping along
             the dead-centre of the road
        we saw no signs of life.

The cathedral.
        Also locked.
Then tuna salad and Peroni
        in a shaded courtyard
                with three metal tables.

At one
        a white cat slept in the only chair.
At the second
        a handsome Capuchin friar
        in brown habit and sandals
        took extremely careful sips of water
                while a woman much younger than himself
                leaned forward and murmured earnestly
                without a single interruption.
The friar
        sometimes nodded
                and took another sip of water.

        At a different time
at the third table
                we might have felt exhausted.
Here we were reconciled.
        Perfectly content
with each other   which made us
content as well   with the confusion of things
        that had brought us here
                and spared us.

We finished our meal.

We wandered off
and found our way
    to the dusty corner where
our bus appeared like a miracle.

With the sun behind us now
    and hills darkening as they swelled
        towards the mouth of their dead volcano
and small fires
    unless they were spirals of mist
    twisting up from the valley floors
we saw our own shadow
    crumpling against the corners
        long before we reached them
and the distance to travel seemed much shorter
    or had already gone.

The Mill

Over the road
and twice the size of the house we lived in
        five stories at least
                white clapboard
                        wide as a barn.

The cat reconnoitred.

I followed the cat
        clambering
                this side or that
of the mounting-block steps
        then ducking the sack
        that drooped like a sleepy eye
        almost to block the door

and in.

Darkness.

                        Light.

Shadows that
                jigged with bran-dust
                and wheat-dust
and softened the pulleys
        the beams
                the ladder fading away
                 towards this attic or that
        where the miller must be
        ignoring me
        on my porridgy floor.

And hushed.

But roaring in fact
        the dry
        continual
        biblical
        thunder
        of mill-wheels
        grinding together.

    Surely
the heaviest weight in the world.

Furious too
with a fury of infinite patience.

    Where was I now?
I'd forgotten.
            No no I remembered.
            Looking for something
    I was
like the cat looking
            here between rows
            and rows of comfortable sacks
            like soldiers asleep.

    Looking for this
            perhaps
                    this handful of grain in a gush
                    overflowing my hands
                    at a rickety funnel
                    like money but free
            and precious   priceless
if only I caught it.

Maybe not this.

Maybe just wanting
     the doorway again
          what with the weight at my back
the weight
     and darkness
breathing and grinding.

Look.

Was that really my home there
over the road?

That acacia tree by the gate.

     That border of pinks.

My mother's face in a window pane
     like a bubble
          frozen in water.

Surely again
     surely
          surely not mine.

Besides
     I had turned into dust.
White hands
     white clothes
          white hair.
And next thing would float away
          through the white air.

Wait

When prayers are over
    I lie in the dark
        I wait
my mother   here
    on the slippery eiderdown
        her
one hand smoothing my hair
        the other
    breathing Blue Fern
from a wet dot on her wrist

and   it is time
        she says   it is time to explain
miracles really
        are not

listen
    the Burning Bush
    it had oily leaves
the Red Sea   that was
    the tides   yes
and Jesus   Jesus
    walking across the water

ah
    but I know about that
already   I know because
    I have fooled my father
already
        I have discovered
this sandbar   lying

        just under the surface
all   invisible
and
        I have walked it already

anyway
        wait
wasn't that   now   downstairs
        my father
home before we expected
                me and my mother
        clearing his throat
                lifting up lids on the stove

yes   and always the same
with him   with him
                it is always time
                        for something
what have I done   what am I
doing   how have I spent
my day

        although   for the moment
here is my mother   still here
        and singing
        the Ugly Duckling
                where at the last
                the very last minute
                he turns

what is a miracle   is it
                the same as a mystery
miracle   mystery
is it   I cannot tell
        what with the surface of water

the endless glittering surface of water
    where I am floating
    where I have fallen
where I am
    under the water and cannot
       is that
my mother still singing
    where is there
wait.

Felling a Tree

It was a Saturday's work in autumn
to fell one ash tree in the copse,
my father handling the buzz-saw
in his cap and boots and windcheater,
me dragging back the undergrowth
then standing clear.

If we were lucky
and he planned it right,
the tree collapsed in one cascading swoop,
and in the aftermath,
with birds in bushes roundabout
returning to their songs again,
we stripped the leaves and twigs away
to have the pale green trunk and branches bare,
reminding me a body can be bare,
before we cut them up as well,
and hauled
the long logs through the brambles to the shed.

*

Back from church next day,
we dusted off
that scarred contraption like a clothes horse
with two Vs on top at either end,
then laid the long logs there
and briskly shortened them
to fit and burn next winter on the fire indoors.

That done,
my father put aside his buzz-saw,
fetched the axe,
worked the whetstone either side until
the blade-edge glittered like a silent scream,
and set to work
with me supplying one log
then another to the gnarly chopping-block

as he swung down,
and he swung down again,
and every one split easily in two,
as though
a law in nature made it happen so.

Laying the Fire

I am downstairs early
looking for something to do

when I find my father on his knees
at the fireplace in the sitting-room
sweeping ash
from around and beneath the grate
with the soft brown hand-brush
he keeps especially for this.

Has he been here all night
waiting to catch me out?
So far as I can tell
I have done nothing wrong.

I think so again
when he calls my name
without turning round;

he must have seen me
with the eyes in the back of his head.

'What's the matter, old boy?
Couldn't sleep?'

His voice is kinder than I expect,
as though he thinks
we have in common a sadness
I do not feel yet.

I skate towards him in my grey socks
over the boards of the sitting-room,
negotiating the rugs
with their patterns of almost-dragons.

He still does not turn round.

He is concentrating now
on arranging a stack of kindling
on crumpled newspaper in the fire-basket,
pressing small lumps of coal
carefully between the sticks
as though he is decorating a cake.

Then he spurts a match,
and chucks it on any old how,

before spreading a fresh sheet of newspaper
over the whole mouth of the fireplace
to make the flames take hold.

Why this fresh sheet
does not also catch alight
I cannot think.

The flames are very close.

I can see them
and hear them raging
through yesterday's cartoon of President Kennedy
and President Khrushchev
racing towards each other in their motorcars
both shouting
I'm sure he's going to stop first!

But there's no need to worry.
Everything
is just as my father wants it to be,
and in due time,
when the fire is burning nicely,
he whisks the newspaper clear,

folds it under his arm,

and picks up the dustpan
with the debris of the night before.

Has he just spoken to me again?
I do not think so. I
do not know.
I was thinking how neat he is.
I was asking myself:
will I be like this? How will I manage?

After that he chooses a log
from the wicker wood-basket
to balance on the coals,
and admires his handiwork.

When the time comes to follow him,
glide, glide over the polished floor,
he leads the way to the dustbins.

A breath of fine white ash
pours continuously over his shoulder
from the pan he carries before him
like a man bearing a gift
in a picture of a man bearing a gift.

The Lych Gate

All Saints, Stisted, August 1900

Thousands of heavily seeded grass-heads
    are waving through the lych gate
I have entered
        countless times
to find the churchyard always trim.

This must be
      because the mower and his scythe
        cannot be spared at harvest time
    besides which
 the dead are not many.

Charles Morgan Forster is here
    and the crafty builder who designed
      the twisted chimneys in the main street
seems to be a recent arrival.

But the dozens of crosses and headstones
    packed on the slope
      down to the river
do not exist yet

and the empty ground by the flint wall
    where my great-grandfather
      and my great-grandmother
        my grandfather
        my mother
      and my father
lie in their descending order

is just that
empty ground

where I have yet to stand and imagine
   the bliss
      of having never been born.

2 LAURELS AND DONKEYS

A Moment of Reflection
28 June 1914

Although one assassin has already tried
and failed to blow him to pieces,
Archduke Ferdinand has let it be known
he will very soon complete his journey
as planned along the quay in Sarajevo,
but for a moment will pause
here,
at the window of a private room in the town hall.

He needs time to recover his composure
after finding the blood of his aide-de-camp
spattered over the manuscript of the speech
he delivered from a nearby balcony earlier this morning.
And indeed,
the prospect of an Austrian brewery in the distance
is reassuring,
likewise the handsome red brick of the barracks
filled with several thousand soldiers of the fatherland.

This is how those who survive him today
will remember him:

a man thinking his thoughts
until his wife has finished her own duties –
the Countess Chotek
with her pinched yet puddingy features,
to whom he will shortly whisper
'Sophie, live for our children',
although she will not hear.

As for his own memories:

the Head of the local tourist bureau
has now arrived and taken it upon himself
to suggest the Archduke might be happy to recall the fact
that only last week
he bagged his three thousandth stag.

Was this, the Head dares to enquire,
with the double-barrelled Mannlicher
made for him especially –
the same weapon he used to dispatch
two thousand one hundred and fifty game birds
in a single day,
and sixty boars in a hunt led by the Kaiser?

These are remarkable achievements
the Head continues,
on the same level as the improvement
the Archduke has suggested in the hunting of hare,
by which the beaters,
forming themselves into a wedge-shape,
squeeze those notoriously elusive creatures
towards a particular spot
where he can exceed the tally of every other gun.

In the silence that follows
it is not obvious whether the Archduke
has heard the question.

He has heard it.

He is more interested, however,
in the memories it brings to mind:
the almost infinite number of woodcock,
pigeon, quail, pheasant and partridge,

wild boars bristling flank to flank,
mallard and teal and geese
dangling from the antlers of stags,
layer after layer of rabbits
and other creatures that are mere vermin –

a haul that he expects will increase
once the business of today has been completed.

In the Stacks

These dry scraps are five olive leaves
Denis Browne pulled from the olive tree
growing over the grave he had just dug

on Skyros for Rupert Brooke in April 1915
and posted back home to Cathleen Nesbitt.
They lie here as brittle and glittering now

as the scales of a surprisingly large fish,
but I think they are what it says they are,
because strange as it might seem I myself

stood under this tree almost fifty years later,
aged seventeen and so beginning to discover
how existence is measured out and must end,

thanks in part to the procession of red ants
marching from a narrow crack in the coping
designed for the grave by Brooke's mother

after Denis Browne had made his farewell
and boarded his ship the *Grantully Castle*,
sailing towards his own death at Gallipoli.

2

Resting in the trench now but this soldier
with his soft cap and kilt, his bare knees
and open wind-nipped face, will disappear

over the top in a moment and so leave behind
the terrier, the jaunty white terrier called Argos
who, if his master returns, will raise his head

because this man smells like the same man
that left all those minutes ago, although to see
the changes in him now no one would think so.

3

What flew in from another land
enraged the sky above the Strand –

an insect like a huge cigar
splashed about with tongues of fire,

with someone crouching at a door
despite our guns' tremendous roar

to drop his clutch of shining bombs
across our dark and quiet homes.

Remember, I was still a child
and never thought I might be killed.

I liked the bombs, I liked the fire,
I liked the huge high-up cigar,

I liked especially how the lights
cut misted pathways through the night

and how my footsteps made no sound
when I walked there, not on the ground.

4

This report is a continuation of one numbered 303A
and contains extracts from letters from Indian soldiers
relating to the fortnight concluded on 13th inst.
Those cited here illustrate how almost impossible it is
for barriers to be effective in Oriental correspondence.

Among several examples showing courage and duty
Orientals excel in the art of conveying their information
without saying anything definite [*words missing here*].
When they have meaning to convey they are apt to use
a phrase such as 'Think it over until you understand it',
or some equivalent. It naturally follows that their news
is exceedingly vague and will give rise to wild rumours.

It has nevertheless been possible to draw some conclusions;
e.g.: the prospect of a return to the firing line appears to be
regarded with something approaching [*words missing here*],
as in: 'My brother, this is no war. It is the final destruction
of the world. A whole world is being killed. If ever I return
I shall tell you very much. If I end here, what is there to tell.'

In the same way, extracts show that the man who has served
and been wounded feels he has amply [*words missing here*],
as in: 'The guns are firing. The Kings are looking on. Like dust
the dead are lying before the trench. Thus are we all sacrificed.'

5

What tree was felled in what remote forest,
then dragged by what engine or elephant
through what jungle to what paper-mill
in what sea-port, then shipped to what dock

then sold how and cut how and brought how
for 2nd Lieutenant Owen on this particular day
in Craiglockhart War Hospital in Edinburgh
to single it out thinking, Now, here, with this

pen on this tabletop with this my right hand
I shall write down these words in this order
to catch what I am trying to say then pass it
along the corridor to him who just happens

to be recovering there from his own troubles,
and who, when not practising his golf swing,
will read them and recommend that one thing
becomes another, for example the word 'dead'

which he thinks should be 'doomed', and also
that 'silent minds' be changed to 'patient minds'?

6

At the very end of everything, the last man emerges
through a copse of trees without any leaves or branches
and comes to a halt on the greasy slope of a bomb-crater

where in a brown puddle he sees his own face looking up
to remind him of the need to wash himself. Laying aside
on the pitted bank his tin hat and satchel, his lousy jacket,

he slithers forward as close as he dare to the water's edge
where mud immediately swallows his boots to the ankle,
spreads his legs while at the same time leaning forward

as if the air itself were solid enough to stop him toppling,
and scoops a dark handful from the pool. The impression,
as he uses his left hand to smear the water over his neck

and jaw, and his right to continue the process over his chin
and mouth, is of a man taking a firm grip of his own face
before twisting his head off the delicate screw of his neck

and rather than washing himself throwing away his skull
along with everything inside it that can never be forgotten
and so, at the very end of everything, become clean again.

The Camp

Near the dogleg turn of the lane down to the ponies' field,
skulking in summer among cow parsley and meadowsweet,
in winter with their streaked black corrugated walls laid bare,
were the half-dozen Nissen huts my father refused to mention.
A prisoner of war camp for Italian soldiers my mother told me,
but also part of the silence my father had brought back with
    him
ten years before from Germany which now could not be ended
although the reason for that was one more thing he never gave.
Why spoil an early morning stroll bringing halters for the
    ponies
so we could lead them home to the stable yard then saddle up?
What else could there possibly be on earth for us to talk about
that was more interesting than a blackbird calling in the hedge,
or the swarming hawthorn flowers that smelled faintly of
    drains,
or the rain cloud that he always said was only a clearing
    shower?

A Pine Cone

In Belsen,

from the flagstone path that swerves
past one mass grave
shaped like a flat-topped Neolithic long-barrow

to the next mass grave,

and wanders too
beside free-standing headstones
bearing individual names or family names,
Anne Frank's among them,
that cannot be placed exactly
where the bodies lie
but remember them,

I brought away a pine cone,
one of thousands darkening the ground.

I carried it home and placed it here
on my windowsill in the open air
and milder English sun.

Now its stiff woody elements,
brown with darker brown fringes,
have turned into a creature
with manifold silent mouths
all stretched open to their fullest extent.

When I pick it up
it is lighter than before,
almost weightless between my fingers
but rustling faintly as I revolve it,

taking me back to the tree that reared above me
with its baked and fissured trunk,

and the stone path I was halfway down,

and the graves I had passed
and those still to come
flattened under their gloss of flowering heather
and spirals of lark song.

Little one. Little
creature abandoned.
Tell me
what should I do next
with your useless beauty.

I breathe. I exclaim
when your brittle weight passes
from my hand onto the windowsill again;

the breeze catches and rolls it,
threatening a fall,

then a moment later drifts idly away
and there you stay.

Finis

Bare facts and staggering multitudes: what hope
what possible hope left for language with finish?
Light. Knock. Road. Engine. Rail. Truck. Cold. Night.
Whatever these words meant, they no longer mean.

*

A conductor's baton twitches to the left or right:
this one has been selected to die, this one not yet.
Clothes. Belt. Shoes. Watch. Ring. Gold tooth. Hair.
Silence is singing instead from the guts of a violin.

*

Not to go mad, or to go mad and understand madness,
to gaze steadily on the world with the eyes of Lazarus.
Lager. Barracks. Bunks. Kapos. Musselmans. Chimney.
The mind cannot skip the air and mingles with smoke.

*

Buried in each, the appearance they still remember
but transparent, with no existence in the others near.
Work. Soup. Mud. Work. Snow. Work. Soup. Gone.
The body is murdered over and over devouring itself.

*

A white plain outside under the flight of the crows
and men standing there like a spinney of withered trees.
Sky. Cloud. Earth. Grass. Bird. Field. Hedge. Wheat.
Prayer rising and God's spittle falling on bare heads.

*

What hope, what possible hope for finish? *My father,*
I wanted to tell you something, but I did not know what.
Language, the tip flickering to and fro, threw out a voice.
A wavering flame . . . like a speaking tongue . . . so I set
   forth . . .

A Tile from Hiroshima

Look at it this way

mud
                sludge
                        sand
scooped from the bay

        a mould
            fired
at a thousand degrees

        glittery green-black
inside the typical
                grey

        and
                dull earth worn underfoot
made
        a roof overhead

                *

Look at it this way

        Democritus coined *atomos*
solid
        unchanging
                particles

then
        two thousand years
                with the vaults of nature
        locked
                and silence in the laboratories

silence on this at least

before
    a shape
        John Dalton
    he gave the idea a shape
a sphere
        a billiard ball
or   millions of billiard balls

and
    every one changeable
        if
                they are left to themselves
with energy   very great energy
    fizzing in space   containing
particles   like

like what
    like marbles
        Rutherford says
or planets
    miniature planets revolving
call them
    the whisper of nature

changeable   yes
    vibrating   yes
and quick to jump
    jumping   from one
    one orbit or shell to another
vibrating like
    like a wave   like what
like violin strings   like what

    continue

look at it this way

Chadwick decides
this
    the neutron   this
    the positron   this
the charged electron
                speeding the particle up
                    smashing them

but
        no chain
    not yet   no nothing
like trying to shoot down birds from the sky
    in the dark
        in a country with
            very few birds

    look at it this way
uranium
        ah
    that is the chain
        beginning
that
    is the heat
        the light
the natural order of things
    interrupted

        that
I may rise
            and stand
                that
and bend your force to break

                *

Look at it this way. From the observation plane flying high
over the city with sunlight rippling along its silver belly

there is a clear view of offices and schools and factories
and wood-frame houses all with roofs of the same dark tiles
fanning over the six flat islands formed by the seven rivers
branching at regular intervals from the principal river the Ota

and a population of two hundred and forty-five thousand souls
including ten thousand enslaved Koreans with the pensioners
already working to make firebreaks in case those are needed
and troops and others digging trenches in the surrounding hills
where they expect to fight to the last man following the invasion
and children tearing up pine roots to make oil for airplane fuel
or moulding fist-sized sand-balls held together by a floury paste
which are intended to be thrown from a safe distance into the fire

and before the plane vanishes from sight also several fine bridges
that even from such a height appear to sway in the salmonish sun
now that a warm front has settled across this part of the Empire
and black water beneath that looks so pure it must be drinkable.

*

Now a second plane also very high
        invisible in fact
            but look at it this way

a Superfortress
        stripped   rewired
            modified

No. 82   *Enola Gay*
for the mother of Commander Tibbets
    since she supported Tibbetts
        when he dropped out of Med School

        and   forty kilometres out
              Captain Lewis adding to his log
                    Everyone has a big hopeful look on his face.

                              *

Look at it this way
      was it a meteor striking

was it a gigantic photograph
      taken by the Americans

was it a Molotov Flower Basket
      made of separate charges

was it the sun falling from the sky

      was it magnesium powder
exploding when it made contact
      with the city power system

was it a new weapon entirely
      a genshi bakudan
the original child bomb.

                  *

              Imagine   at least imagine
                    a bell-shape in the air
                        a dome-shape
              dead centre   beneath the detonation

                  and the flash   the blast
              rushing out   through streets above
                    sewers
                        below ground

              and
                    the bodies of the population

look at it this way
        a bell-shape
and roof tiles on every house
        where
every house stood
        like fish scales   melting

not melting quite
            glossy
        glossy and slipping
            down slipping
down through fire
        ash   ghost
            nothing
to sweat there.

                *

Look at it this way   no longer
the roof overhead and sparrows arguing there
but a tile weeping in the dustbowl of the house

                            no longer
the breakfast ration of rice steaming on a table
but a still-unripe pumpkin roasted on the vine

                            no longer
the shadow patrolling among water lily leaves
but a carp poached belly-up in its own juices

                            no longer
the X-ray plate lying undeveloped in the in-tray
but the same plate printed with a pure whiteness

                            no longer
the rush hour traffic stalled crossing a bridge
but hundreds of mangled bicycles without tyres

                              no longer
a rain shower sweeping down from a low cloud
but moisture-drops with the weight of marbles

                              no longer
a doctor among ruins handing out good advice
but Excuse me for having no burden like yours

                              no longer
men women and children walking towards you
but the skin slithering from their hands and faces
but burn-prints of metal buckles and suspenders
but eye sockets empty because eyes have melted.

                    *

          Look at it
              this way
          here is Dr Bronowski   what
              is he doing
                  here in the rubbish

          here among weeds
                  the weeds
              that spring from ashes
          the bluets   and Spanish bayonets
              goosefoot
                  the morning glories
          day lilies
              feverfew
                      panic grass   panic
          grass   feverfew   glories

          he is collecting   he is
              choosing this tile from the ruins
                  he knows
          what does he know

he knows
    a tile of this type
is locally used   melting point
    thirteen hundred degrees

what else
    he knows *the ascent of man*
he thinks   he knows
    how one thing
        becoming another thing
in the ascent
    descends

and
    senna he knows
        sickle senna
    so much   so many
here at the centre   the eye
    the plane
        might almost have dropped it
            almost

but senna
    dropped from a plane
the very idea

            look at it this way
here
    though burned
        though fired to a deeper black
a glossier black
    in the melting

here
    with feverfew
panic grass   panic grass

here is the tile
the tile which jumped to his hand
and settled
and settled
surviving

look at it
this way.

The Fence

I found my way home but it was not until summer
ended that my mother brought herself to ask me
to make good the fence that marks our boundary.
I went out there with a box of nails and a hammer
and when a flock of crows in the trees surrounding
made some comment, I remembered how the birds
living by Shamash Gate spoke in perfect harmony
with mortar shells falling. Then I began knocking
nails into the wood and everything near took fright
although not my mother, who continued watching
from her chair on the porch. I have said nothing yet
of what it is like to reach the exact point where one
place becomes another, with no way forward or back,
and there is nothing else left to do except fall down.

Peace Talks

1 *War Debts*

I started
living with Debbie when I was fifteen,
but I was never the best-behaved boy in school
so obviously she had a bit of a battle there.

Then I went to college but I sacked that,

so my sister's boyfriend
he asked me
have you thought about joining the army,
and I told him
I've not
but I will now,
and next thing there I was
doing my Phase One at Purbright,
then Lark Hill
the rolling plains.

We knew
right
we knew we were going out,
and it was like,
guys,
this is going to be tough.

Did you know Camp Bastion is the size of Reading?
I didn't know.
And ninety-five degrees with your body armour.

You wonder how they miss you to be honest,
throwing their stuff over the walls.

But they do miss you
most of the time.
One of my mates, he got hit, though,
I say hit,
by a shower of Afghan fingers.

Suicide bomber in the road outside.

Normally the alarm gets you first
but even then you'll be
wow,
wow,
something is real.

My friends at home
can't understand what I'm saying.
It's the anticipation I'm used to.
It's the news I'm waiting to hear.
No rumours.
Everyone quiet and waiting for the facts.

Surreal if I'm honest.
Surreal when I get back.

The ease. The slow pace.

In Subway, for instance.
Cucumbers. Tomatoes.
You think:
Get it done *now*, so everyone can go.
Just *come on*!

Then you leave
and road works are everywhere
with nothing moving.
And rain pattering down
and clouds covering the stars.

The war debts will come out then.
You think:
my weapon
where is my weapon?
And you look for it.
You did everything with your weapon
and urgh
you miss it.
Nobody understands.
You miss it.
You went to the toilet with it.
And the shower with it.
You went running with it.
You did everything with it.
If you had a doss bag,
you kept it close as you could,
or in your doss bag
sort of thing.

It's trust, you see,
you have to trust your weapon.
It's individual.

I'm Stephen North.
Lance Bombardier Stephen North.

2 *Ficklety*

This time we were looking at transition, the next incarnation.
It's interesting. Soldiers carry a lot on their hats you know,
and we talk together about sadness, the ficklety of mortality.

One man, he was always getting sand out of his nose and ears,
and as more sand came to him, more and more sand and dust,
he counted it, he knew how many grains of sand there were.

As for me, I read the Psalms. The wilderness. The helplessness.
The rocks, stones, wind and thorn trees. I encountered them all.
But a dog collar? No. Collar crosses instead and a tactical flash.

Then I came home and here are my children and my little list:
roof needs fixing, grass needs a cut, the long green grass,
we need such and such for the kitchen, bathroom, everywhere,

and aah I've wrapped the car round a tree, aah. It's interesting.
Now I think we are beginning to see the bow-wave of trauma.
Therefore I go with the men sometimes, pray for them always.

3 *Life So Far*

My mother was keen to celebrate birthdays –
still is.
When I turned twenty-five
I got her cake on exercise in Brecon,
my friend Tom
pulled it out from his rucksack for me –
he'd been carting it round a week.

Then I got cake again
in the Mess before we went to head off.

Afghanistan is something I wanted,
really wanted.
I've always enjoyed being outside,
playing in the woods.

First job
was Ground Holding in Central Helmand,
a base the size of a tennis court,
fifteen people,
actually good
for someone who doesn't have a house so far
or anything.

We patrolled a lot on foot,
maybe eight or ten hours each day;
if you think of the country
like a map of the Underground
we were pretty safe in Zones 1 and 2.
Further off in Zone 4
it was more kinetic,

which I'd say refers to enemy action
when they're shooting at you,
a good insurgent presence.

After that
we went to the desert country west of Sangin,
a thousand metres above sea level,
absolutely bare and cold.
At night I dug this hole
only a little larger than my body;
I was very cosy in my down jacket,
with a warm sleeping bag,
and a thick mat.

I was making a nest,
everything tucked in.

It's a strange one.
All night I was just a pair of eyes
with the sky running over me,
not sleeping,
looking at the stars and the black horizon,
not seeing any depth.
There's something to be said
for thinking earth has been here a long time.
Everything feels sweeter
coming back to camp after that.

Trees for instance.
And poppy fields in April and May –
field after field of poppies –
then desert,
then more blocks of colour,
pink and red and white.
And compounds showing up green,

and clear blue skies
above brown walls and barbed wire.

Really quite good actually:
you've made your decision,
you want to lead men in an operation.
But you don't want to die,
not much,
so you're always looking for ground signs,
a patch of disturbed earth,
a wire poking out
or an antenna,
and you're always totally unpredictable
about where you are,

erratic,

finding the most difficult way
to get to anywhere,
avoiding bottlenecks and crossroads,
cutting through hedges,
constantly observing,
in and out of the ditches which were –.

Well,
you're carrying fifty kilos of equipment,
wearing body armour plates front and rear,
smaller ones on both sides,
knee-pads, gloves, glasses, helmet, chin-strap,
ear-piece for the radio,
thick lycra shorts to protect against the blast,
also a heavy thing like a nappy.

Amazing how the body gets used to it.

You sweat and sweat
and you don't hold anything back,
you just sweat and accept.

Once a week
we went down to Helmand River,
cliffs one side
and the other a wide green zone,
and no we didn't swim there,
the current was too fast.

But we did stand there in our full armour,
and we saw the country opening
right the way up to the mountains.

Another time
it was four o'clock in the morning,
June,
and we needed to cross a ditch,
actually much less of a ditch
more like a river,
a narrow river and straight,
with trees either side
and the moon shining between them.

I stepped forward.

I stepped forward into the water
and I felt
my feet lose
touch with the bottom,
and I was just
'O goodness I'm sinking',
and my legs were floating away
but it was all fine

to get wet,
it was fine,
and go through onto the high ground again.

4 *The Programme*

I'm an army brat. I was brought up
to love the army. Basically I now do
army intelligence work. I'm twenty.

It was difficult for Mum to start with.
Take good care of yourself she said;
keep your head down; be a grey man.

But you can't do that, no. You see it.
You see it and you think it isn't real,
until you get smells and other things.

I miss the gym, did I mention the gym?
I did the Insanity Training Programme
and I loved it. I followed that through.

5 *Talking to the Moon*

Twenty-two years   I've been in the army
my husband
we were at Sandhurst together
and five years after

courting
I think is the word

I'd done Bosnia by then
in a tented camp
with the floods
and guys ringing home
with water
up to their knees

so with his tours
in Ireland
Iraq
Afghanistan now
I do understand
I do
I've been there
I've done that

but hey
I don't want to hear

the day
he sent me a bluey
I took it
I looked at the map

mistake
a giant mistake
I thought
don't need it
I don't

we have four children
and Freddy the oldest
fourteen
he's quick
much quicker

stop
stop
stop
stop

I set up the choir

I've started my art

you have to do something

Sharon and Franny and Pam

I don't know
what would I do

injured

or broken

also there's writing
but actually
I am so

hey
at least you're twisting the lid

or
you look at the mountains
they take you away

who could be there

who has explored them

who
is living there now

also the sky

if the children
are wanting to talk
I say to them
talk to the moon
Daddy can do that

talk to the moon together

then there's the bunting

it's hardly
like Christmas
but listen
it comes with us everywhere

we have a box

embarrassing really
never mind that
no one will see it
this time

this time when he's home
we're tucked away in the woods.

6 *Critical Care*

Jesus – Stay still – Stay fucking still –

Stay with us – Put morphine on it –

Don't touch it – Don't touch it –

We've got to get him out now –

We've got to get him out now –

*

All the way across on the slide.
Everyone ready?
Slide

*

You're back in England.
and my name's Clare.
You've got three of us you lucky boy.
Kate, and Hazel, and Clare.

Now just take a little break
in your breathing again.

Good lad, good lad,
you're doing very well.

But it's not the best day you've ever had,
is it, Andrew?

*

The explosion has driven
a whole load of sand
and mud and rubbish
up into the tissue planes.

And of course the bugs,
they've got in there
and they love it.

They've got a lovely warm moist wound,
lots of nutrients,
and they think they're on holiday.

*

This is Mum,
Mum's come to see you.

And Natalie was on the phone
asking how you're doing.

She's waiting for me to tell her
everything's all right.

But it's not, is it babes?

Well,
we'll wait for the morning
and see how that goes.

*

We're going to try and save the other leg,
his foot still has a pulse.

We're going to use topical negative pressure,
suction if you like, or a vacuum.

The bugs really don't like it.

*

If you knew what was in store for you
you wouldn't have your children.

*

The blast also ripped the gums from his teeth.
This thing here,
this is a bit of grass from an Afghan field.

*

Natalie's with me now.

She says the baby's
kicking the crap out of her,
don't you love?

*

The surface of his eyes are so badly burned
a special membrane has been imported from America
to help reduce scarring.

It's the best chance he has
of regaining some sight.

*

Now
is really a waiting game.

All you do is wait.

*

Unfortunately
the foot doesn't look very good.

Dusky.

The decision to operate depends on several factors.

    *

I told you I'd be back to hold your hand,
didn't I, love?
Here I am. I hope you can feel me holding.

    *

Sister could you get a power amputation saw?

An amputation saw on power?

    *

I imagine his first thoughts will be
it's better off dying.

    *

As long as you can sleep peacefully
after making the decision
then you have made the right decision.

And I think we will sleep peacefully
after making this decision today.

    *

We find on the whole
when we do take the station off,
and allow them to wake up,
they are absolutely terrified.

Then we keep having to stress
they are safe now.
They are safe now.

*

It's all looking good.

It's all looking very good in fact.

What we do next is take a sliver of skin,
a graze,
like when you fall off your bike.

Can I give you the skin?

*

You are sort of coming round now,
aren't you love?

You've been here three weeks
and you've been injured.

Yes lovey you have.

You've been here three weeks
and I've been at your side.

You've been injured.

*

He's been nodding yes and no
and squeezing my hand.

I can't tell
what the noes are about.

*

You still remember what's wrong don't you?

No?

You want to hear again?

You've lost your legs.

Yes two of them, both of them.

Please don't push me away, mate.
Please don't push me away.

*

Andrew lives every day.

He lives every day for a hopefully.

7 *One Tourniquet*

It was a long time ago
but I was there,
a combat medical technician.

I saw
children and IEDs
which wasn't nice at all.

One boy:
he had shorts and a dirty vest,
he stood on a mine.

He was conscious at first,
screaming,

and I thought
what a mess.

All in a bit of field.

None of the other kids cried,
they're all quite sort of tough.

Very tough kids in fact.

Definitely.

At the time
we were issued with only one tourniquet each.

But Camp Phoenix was down the road
and he went there.

A double amputee.

We heard later he survived.

So yeah. Brilliant.

Everything is hard.
Everything they've got to do
everywhere they've got to go.
Just hard.

I used to imagine
little towns in the country
nobody knew.

Little towns nobody had touched.

People would be living there
all the same.

Just living there
in the vastness.

8 *The Gardener*
   In memory of Lieutenant Mark Evison

We spent
many hours kneeling together in the garden
      so many hours
            Mark
he liked lending a hand

watching *Gardeners' World*

building compost heaps

or the brick path with the cherry tree
that grows over it now   the white cherry
      where I thought   I mustn't cry
I must behave
      as if he's coming back

      *

It was just after Easter
with everything in leaf

      he is so sweet really
            though worldly
                  before his time

I kissed him and said
                  See you
in six months   and he turned

      he turned and said

      *

I opened the garden for the first time

the National Gardens Scheme
        you know
                what gardens are like in May

and this man was hovering around
        outside the front

as we walked down the side passage
        he said
                I'm a Major

I said   Oh my son   he's in the army
        sort of brightly

        *

Then no one was there

so I went
                and I gardened all day

how slow   how satisfying

I felt next morning
                he was struggling for his life

        *

He would be home
        with three transfers
                on three different planes

my daughter Elizabeth and I drove to Birmingham
my mobile   there   on the dashboard

we had worked out the times of the last plane
and we arrived

and they still hadn't called me
  and he was still

*

He was lying   he was
with this
    Mark
with this big plastic hole
    sort of
a bandage over a hole
    just like
asleep

*

The reindeer   the wild reindeer
    giving birth in the snow
        with the rest of the herd scarpering

they have seen the eagle above them

but the mother stands still
    what am I going to do   what

a bit restless   and everything
    but starting to lick her baby
with the eagle   watching

*

Quietened   that is the best word
to describe it   I felt quietened
seeing the hills below
    as we came into Kabul

I was thinking

Mark lived in a very green place
and here everything is purple
        orange   Turner colours I call them

in my nightmares he is never dead
bandaged   lost   never dead
with my love
            circling
        nowhere to go

I was thinking

                thousands of lives
                        in an instant
and the molecules starting again

        and the mountains never changing

how was I
        quietened
                    how

but for a moment
        I was
then losing height
        with the brown earth rushing to meet me.

Acknowledgements

Thanks are due to the editors of the following, in which most of these poems have already appeared: *Ambit, Best British Poetry 2014* (Salt), *Echo Chamber* (Radio 4), *Granta, Guardian, London Review of Books, Mimic Octopus, Observer, Ploughshares* (USA), *Poem, Poetry and All That Jazz, 1914: Poetry Remembers, The Spectator* and *Times Literary Supplement.*

In 'The Death of George Mallory and Sandy Irvine' I gratefully use material from *Into the Silence* by Wade Davis (Bodley Head, 2011), by permission of the author and the Random House Group Ltd.

'Finis' was commissioned by the Revd Dr James Hawley, precentor of Westminster Abbey, and read at a service there on 1 February 2015 to commemorate the 70th anniversary of the liberation of Auschwitz. I acknowledge the use of material from *A Lucky Child* by Thomas Buergenthal, *Man's Search for Meaning* by Viktor E. Frankl, *If This is a Man* by Primo Levi and *Night* by Elie Wiesel.

'A Tile from Hiroshima' was commissioned by the Imperial War Museum (North). I acknowledge the use of material from *Hiroshima* by John Hersey and *Hiroshima Nagasaki* by Paul Ham.

The poems in 'In the Stacks' were commissioned by Poet in the City and the London Archives, and were written in response to items in the British Library.

'The Fence' uses material from *The Yellow Birds* by Kevin Powers, copyright © Kevin Powers 2012. Reproduced by permission of the author c/o Rogers, Coleridge & White Ltd, 20 Powis Mews, London W11 1JN.

'Peace Talks' was broadcast in a slightly different form on Radio 4 on 11 November 2014, under the title 'Coming Home'.

Several of the poems in this collection, like others in my previous collection, *The Customs House* (2012), have their origins in other people's books or words, and often borrow from and/or adapt them. I gratefully acknowledge the following: for 'The Discoveries of Geography', *A History of the World in Twelve Maps* by Jerry Brotton; for 'The Conclusions of Joseph Turrill', *An Oxfordshire Market Gardener*, ed. Eve Dawson and Shirley Royal; for 'A Meeting of Minds with Henry David Thoreau', *Walden* and *Journals* by Henry David Thoreau; for 'A Moment of Reflection', *Black Lamb and Grey Falcon* by Rebecca West.

The poems in the second part of this book belong with my series of poems about twentieth- and twenty-first-century Western wars, *Laurels and Donkeys*, several of which were included in *The Customs House*. One day I hope they will join them in a single gathering.

The poems in 'Peace Talks' are based on conversations with soldiers and their relatives. I am very grateful to the following: Lance Bombardier Stephen North ('War Debts'); Padre David Anderson and Sharon Anderson ('Ficklety'); Adjutant Michael Altenhoven ('Life So Far'); Lance Corporal Ben Johnson ('The Programme'); Major Wendy Faux ('Talking to the Moon'); Ranger Andrew Allen, Linda Allen, Chris Allen, Major Clare Dutton, Lt. Col. Steve Geoffrey, Senior Care Nurse Erica Perkins, and everyone associated with the 2009 BBC TV programme *Wounded* ('Critical Care'); Sergeant Vicky Clarke ('One Tourniquet'); Dr Margaret Evison ('The Gardener').